"There is no ground of existence that does not require (or fail to sustain) its poet. This proposition, requiring continual re-proving, has found again its confirmation in Edgar Kunz's first book. In the lineage of Levine, Jordan, and Laux, *Tap Out* presents the data of blows received and taken in fully. Yet these poems do not return blow for blow; they offer instead an unflinching, continued allegiance to abiding connection. Without summation or comment, they remind us that all alchemies of being are possible. Kunz's precision-tool language of memory and witness enlarges, pivots, pieces together the broken into a world made new, survivable, holdable, forgiven."

— Jane Hirshfield, author of
The Beauty and *Come, Thief*

"The sustained lyricism of these poems is all the more powerful for being burned at the edges by memory, by grief, by regret. In terms of craft, this poetry creates a world where human action reaches language the way gravity bends starlight: in a drama of weight and light. This is a hard-pressed place, a territory of failed relationships and regions that never becomes landscape. As its reporter, Edgar Kunz lives up to its challenges and understands its limits. This is a wonderful first book, memorable and unsettling."   — Eavan Boland, author of
A Woman Without a Country

"Edgar Kunz's startling debut, *Tap Out,* is one of the best books of poetry I've read in a long time. These poems interrogate what is received and what is bequeathed in our damaged systems of masculinity, and they do so in ways that are unexpectedly vulnerable. At the same time, the poems are onomatopoeia of humility and busted machismo. It's as if the poems themselves are surprised by how much harm has been done, how much energy and emotion have been expended simply surviving inside of our toxic patriarchy. Fathers are complicit. Friends and brothers are complicit. The speaker is complicit, too, and yet the poems do their vital work without soapboxing. They search constantly for better ways of being human. These are essential poems."

— Adrian Matejka, author of
The Big Smoke and *Map to the Stars*

TAP OUT

TAP OUT

Poems

Edgar Kunz

A MARINER ORIGINAL

HOUGHTON MIFFLIN HARCOURT

BOSTON   NEW YORK   2019

hmhco.com

Library of Congress Cataloging-in-Publication Data
Names: Kunz, Edgar, author.
Title: Tap out : poems / Edgar Kunz.
Description: Boston : Mariner Books/Houghton Mifflin Harcourt, 2019. |
"A Mariner Original."
Identifiers: LCCN 2018033158 (print) | LCCN 2018033745 (ebook) |
ISBN 9781328518132 (ebook) | ISBN 9781328518125 (hardcover)
Classification: LCC PS3611.U59 (ebook) |
LCC PS3611.U59 A6 2019 (print) | DDC 811/.6—dc23
LC record available at https://lccn.loc.gov/2018033158

Book design by Greta D. Sibley

Printed in the United States of America
DOC 10 9 8 7 6 5 4 3 2 1

For Noah and Luke,
my brothers

CONTENTS

TAP OUT

After the Hurricane

Three hundred

miles north, my father beds down in a van by the Connecticut River.
Snow tires rim-deep in the silt. He has a wool horse blanket

tacked inside the windshield. A pair of extra pants bunched
into a pillow. He has a paper bag of partially smoked butts.

A Paw Sox cap. A Zippo. He has state-sponsored cell phone minutes
and a camo jacket hung on the sideview to dry. He can see the Costco

parking lot through the trees. Swelling and emptying out. He wants
to fix things with his wife. He wants a couch to crash on.

He wants a drink. He wants sex. He has a few cans of kidney beans
and a tin of ShopRite tuna. Wrinkled plastic piss bottles line the dash.

Sometimes he walks out to the river and lets the wind sift his lank
and matted hair. Sometimes he peels his socks and stands

in the murky current and thinks about his wife. The birthmark
on her neck. Her one toe longer than the others. Her freckled hands.

He tries to hold her hands in his mind. He tries to remember
the birth years of his sons. He tries to make sense of the papers

he signed. The icy water wetting the hem of his pants. The river stones
sharp underfoot. The wind. I hold him like this in my mind

all afternoon.

In the Supply Closet at Illing Middle

Mike pins me to the sink, forearm
      levered against my throat, flexing
            the needle-nose pliers in one hand.

He and Ant examine the hole in my head
      where the pencil lead snapped off, blood
         leaking down my temple

and pooling in my ear. I squirm
      and Mike presses harder. *Hold still.*
        I know how to do this.

I know what he means: our fathers
      used to salvage wrecks in Mike's sideyard.
        Hammer out the paneling,

clean the fouled spark plugs
      with spit. Flip them for cash or drive them
        until the transmission seized.

If they didn't know where
        one came from, they pulled it
                into the garage, sold it off quick.

Now, Ant stands lookout
        in the doorway. Half-watching
                for teachers and half-watching Mike,

who rinses my hair
        with floor cleaner thick
                as motor oil. Eases my head

toward the weak light
        of the pull-chain bulb. Presses
                the pliers to my skull, and starts to dig.

Free Armchair, Worcester

He pinches the j between his first two fingers squints an eye against the ribbon of smoke sliding up and over his cheekbone. It's me my buddy Ant and Ant's stepdad Randy a half-ass house painter who's always trying to hit us up for weed or pills even though we're thirteen and don't do pills or have any idea how to get them. We're driving Randy's work van into Worcester to pick up a recliner he found in the free section of the Globe. Ant hates his guts and I don't like him much either but Ant's always doing stuff for me like asking his mom if I can stay the night or sneaking me empanadas when my dad doesn't come home so I go along Ant up front me in the back bracing myself against the wheelwells trying not to get knocked around too bad. Randy pulls up in front of the house and we try stuffing the armchair in the back but the arms are too wide. We flip it on one end heave it onto the roof. Lash it down with a tangle of rope from the glovebox and step back. It's not a bad-looking chair. Fabric ratty at the edges but sturdy. Mostly clean. Randy twists another j to celebrate and buys us sandwiches. We post up in an Arby's parking lot the three of us cracking jokes Randy belting folk songs in Spanish. Recliner strapped to the van like a prize buck. He flicks the roach into the weeds says but you skinny-asses you little faggots you could barely lift it and we stop laughing. I look over at Ant and he's sort of picking at his jeans face tight like he got caught doing something dumb like he's ashamed or something and for a second it's like what's gonna happen has already happened. Like the rope's already snapped the armchair gone headlong into the road behind us. Like we're pulled off on the shoulder Randy punching the wheel calling us dumbfucks fuckheads sons-of-bitches sending us out to wait for a lull in traffic and drag the wreckage to the median. Like we've already started to say what we'll say over and over: We knew the whole time. Chair was too heavy. Rope too frayed. Too thin. Nah we knew. No shit we knew. You think we're stupid?

The First Time

Me and Ant shirtless at the corner of Sanford
and St. Paul, straddling our bikes, watching Daryl
pace bowlegged in the gutter – *Yeah man, I mean,
you wouldn't* believe *this chick, man* – scuffing
at the No Dumping plate epoxied to the curb
with the toe of his high-top – *It was like nothing
I ever felt* – Ant and me following the jut of the older
boy's chin to what looks like a popped balloon
lying slack at the bottom of the storm drain.
Nineteen ninety-nine and the most brutal summer
on record, the water ban parching every ball field
statewide. The old men who play rummy
in the shade of a stunted maple have folded up
their lawn chairs and gone inside. The street
is mostly empty – just stillness and heat
and Daryl going on about this girl who just moved
to town and has *tits like this* – a girl who doesn't
know about Daryl yet, his conquest complex
and his big mouth – a girl who doesn't know yet
about this town, the legless vets hanging around
the Army-Navy catcalling public school girls,
the True Gospel Pentecostal women handing out

pamphlets in denim skirts and turtlenecks, the fake
fifties diner on Middle Turnpike where kids get blitzed
in the parking lot and fistfight until the cops show up.
I mean it when I say I'm thirteen and already sick
to death of this place, sick of Daryl, his acned swagger,
the scuff of his hand-me-down Nikes on the curb.
But when Ant taps my shoulder and turns to go,
I don't move. I stand here at the corner, a quick ride
from home, the still-slick condom catching light
in the storm drain, the blacktop radiating heat.
I lay my bike on its side. I step closer to get a good look.

Natick

Windshield smeared with dust. Sun bedded down
in the hills. Drum of my father's hand on the dash startling

the box-nails in the ashtray. Stub he held delicately in his teeth.
Silence we passed back and forth between us, like a joke.

Knowing one day we would stop speaking for good. Knowing it
when the freeway cut ahead of us and Natick fell away

on either side. When he held up his hand to mine, palm
to palm. Nail beds packed with grease. Knuckles more scar

than skin. When he said I had piano hands,
and I was ashamed, and hid them in the pockets of my coat.

Again

Tell me how she left
that morning early left
& you two towns
over hoisting the brush-
rod all day leaning
ladder to brick & me
rapt in the crib quiet
as anything quiet
as something said
almost out loud how
you cupped my skull
in refrigerator light
groped for the whole
milk jar of tomato
how for years
after you'd startle
awake and hover
your hand to feel
for the small fact
of my breathing
though I won't pick up
for you anymore though

what's left is mostly
shame & damaged
light tell me lean
your head into
your shoulder whisper
into your hands

Brothers

Camp Yawgoog
Rockville, Rhode Island

Lift the lid of Rico's steamer trunk
at the foot of the bunkbeds we shared
and it was all laid out, unhidden.
My glove signed by Juan Peña.
My hip-hop tapes. The headlamp
I made out of a bandana and a bike light.
The *Hustler* I stole from my uncle.
Mornings I'd take back what was mine
and each night more would go missing.
Wool socks and a monkey fist. A roll
of camo duct tape. We worked the dining hall,
sweeping up food and bleaching tables.
He told me he was from Worcester
and pulled up his shirt to show the crease
in his belly where he said he was stabbed
by his brother on Farrar Avenue.
Said it didn't even hurt until later.
Told the cops it was a stranger that did it.
It went like that for the rest of the summer,
him stealing and me stealing back
when he wasn't around. When I found
the cashbox from the front office

stuffed in with his underwear – told him
I knew about it, told him it wasn't right –
he called me *family*. Called me *brother*.
Said he knew he didn't have to worry about me.
Gripped my hand and pulled me close.

Workbench

We built it out of scrap wood pulled
from the dumpster next door,

four pressure-treated legs nailed
to a plywood sheet and propped

against a larch in the sideyard.
That winter, the Wilsinski house

had burned down. The fire swelled
above the power lines, singeing the dark

fir trees and making the block reek
of burnt plastic and insulation.

By day, men in baggy jeans
and face masks gutted the single

story ranch, trucked in drywall
and pallets of gypsum brick.

At night, we took what we needed:
three boys slipping under

the chainlink fence, passing
a flickering Maglite over the yard,

looking for the gleam of metal,
roofing tiles, fresh lengths of pine

and vinyl siding we carried back
in our arms. I can't remember, now,

what we were making. If we ever
made a single useful thing.

Mostly, I remember pounding nails
into the larch with a two-by-four.

If one bent, I hammered it sideways
until it went flat, until it was flush

with the bark. Then kept hammering.
My hand going numb, starting to feel

like someone else's hand.

Tap Out

We were vicious. Swollen cheekbones, bruised jaws.
Forearms chafed raw and weeping. The Boston
Crab. The Texas Cloverleaf. The Cross-
Face Chicken Wing. One time, Ant wrenched
my shoulder so hard I couldn't lift my arm
for a week. Another time, Mike's brother Daryl tried
a front-flip slam off the back steps, landed
face-first in the dirt. Wrist bone shot clear
through the skin and gleaming. Mike's dad worked
second shift at Pratt, so if we were loud he'd holler
out the bedroom window, but there was nothing
he could do to punish us we weren't already doing
to each other. And we knew it. Like that time
Daryl showed us his pistol, a .22 he lifted
from a friend's house. We passed it around,
weighing it in our palms. It was heavier
than it looked, but it felt good. He put the barrel
in his mouth and when we jumped up
he laughed and laughed. *Priceless!* he said red-faced
and gasping. *You pussies almost wet your pants!*
We learned new moves, new ways to shock the body
into miracles of pain. The Figure-Four Lock.

The Vise Grip. Every muscle trembling.
The Tarantula. The Camel Clutch. Mouth
pressed against their ear, hissing *Tap out dickhead*
you're not getting out of this you're mine kid
tap out and it'll stop. The Sharpshooter.
The Hammerlock. That sour-hot breath in your ear
and knowing you won't give in, you won't give him
the satisfaction, even when it hurts more
than anything, more than your dad's belt
blistering your backside, more than the night
when Daryl put that gun in his mouth and the sound
of it woke the whole block, so much you grit
your teeth against the pain, sharp kneecap
bearing down on your chest, elbow torqued
past its limit, and you swear you could bust out
of yourself and look down at your body, helpless
and small and trembling, press your mouth
to your own ear and whisper *Not you. Not you.*

Deciding

Not the sirens. Not the men
        dragging canvas, the canceled-
                out moon, the ash windblown

and snarling in our hair. Not
        the sick crack of the ridge beam
                or the gun-clapped silence

after. Not the four of us, brothers
        and our sometimes father,
                our breath knit and drifting,

our useless hands. I mean
        when I lift Noah, half-asleep,
                to my chest and turn

for home. When I look up
        at the windows of our own house
                and see the flames

cold and writhing
in the glass. That first time
I say it out loud: *I'm*

gonna go. And the slow walk
up the drive. And my brother
growing heavy

in my arms.

Graduation

When you showed up drunk as hell, humming
tunelessly to yourself, and slumped against
the auditorium's faux-wood paneling – when
you fumbled in the pockets of your coat,
fished out a cigarette, brought it to your lips,
then, realizing for the first time where you were,
tossed it away and said *Fuck it* loud enough
that everyone turned in their seats and a friend
elbowed me and asked if I knew you – I shook
my head and spent the next hour wondering why
I was so glad you came. You, who slept
each night in your battered van, who skipped
meetings and lied to your sponsor, who still
called your ex-wife every day, restraining order
be damned. You shouldn't have been there
either: a hundred yards was the agreement
after you gathered all the meds in the house
into a shoebox and threatened to take them.
You had come regardless. You were there.
And I was there. And when I walked the stage
you hollered my name with a kind
of wild conviction, then said it a second time,

less convinced, and I thought of that night
when the cops came and you, unashamed
of the fuss you caused, of your desperate,
public struggle for happiness, kissed me
on the head – once, twice – and went quietly.

Blue

Because Craig Mathis fell two stories
through the skylight over the dining room

and lay face-up on the wood floor me
and the other waitstaff waxed on Sundays,

and because the sprinkler pipes tore out
of the ceiling when he fell, tripping

the fire alarm and spraying salt water
over the place settings and chairs, the siren

pealing over every speaker in that
tinderbox hotel with its sheetrock walls

packed with newspaper, and because all
the guests were rushed to the granite

breakwater that divides New Hampshire
from Maine and connects our island

to the island named for the man
who wrecked his ship discovering it,

it took near two hours for someone
to find him there, sprawled on his back

in a Metallica shirt and jeans, hauling in
ragged breaths and murmuring

to himself, and another hour before
the helicopter touched down in the yard

and the EMTs loaded him onto a gurney
and flew him to Boston General.

When Craig came back the next summer,
he limped into the front office

with a different face, a quad-cane
he carried everywhere, a jaw that clicked

when he talked. He said he didn't know
why he was on the roof in the first place.

Said he was glad he couldn't remember.
And so the rest of us needed

to imagine it: that bright instant
before the fall, and the long time

after, having gone through the skylight
and sprawled on his back on the waxed

and polished floor – to wonder
if he looked up at the ruptured piping

and splintered glass, if he understood
it was the route his body took when it left

the charted world, if he saw with his one
undamaged eye the rails of sunlight

and the salt water pouring down,
the framed sky, not a single cloud in it.

Graffiti

Baltimore Rescue Mission
Fairmount and Central

I saw it on the drive up to the farm yesterday
and I see it again this morning: SCUM

in fat bubble letters. White paint livid
on the blacked-over brick. Six thirty and a line

to the middle of the block – looks like
ordinary folks, mostly. Tired, sure. Hungry.

A little embarrassed. How my brothers and I
must have looked waiting outside Social Services

while our father went in to sign up for stamps.
Squatting on the curb, hoping we didn't see

anyone we knew, certain everyone was looking.
No one was looking. Nobody looks

at me now, idling at the light, or at the tag,
or at each other, even – heads down,

shuffling toward the double doors that open
on rows of lawn chairs and folding tables,

plastic placemats the color of bleach.
When we ran the cattle yesterday morning,

herd of Herefords raised for beef, it was
my first time, but I recognized the sharp flanks,

the hunger and fear that moves them
from one chewed-up pasture to another.

When Dad finally came out, he had a look
we couldn't figure. He told the three of us

to stay put, then went and sat by himself
in the truck. The day before, someone had taken

a claw hammer to the steering column
and sped off with a bed full of tools –

table saw, air compressor, everything. The cops
found it abandoned, empty, on the interstate.

He seemed leaner then, and dangerous.
We knew better than to speak. We practiced

hocking loogies. We took a chunk
of concrete to the side of the building,

carved our names into the flaking paint.
Then a few dirty words we knew. I'm at the light

long enough now to see the line swell to the end
of the block and disappear around the corner.

Listening to the tick of the engine.
Wondering if our names are still back there.

When we stood, a few of us, at both ends
of Rayville Road, waving off cars and driving

the cattle up toward the far pasture,
I watched a calf shuffle by. Same as the others,

but with a white spray across his flank.
Crude lettering – some local kids,

I guessed. Names, or cusses. Something violent
and proud. Something about hunger.

My Father at 49, Working the
Night Shift at B&R Diesel

There's no one left to see his hands
        lifting from the engine bay, dark and gnarled
                as roots dripping river mud,

no one to see how his palms – slabs of callus
        from scouring the long throats of chimneys,
                hauling mortar and brick – move

in the fabricated light. Thumb-knuckle
        thick and white as a grub where the box-
                cutter bit. Split nail grown back

scalloped and crooked. The stitch-
        puckered skin. And when they fold into and out
                of themselves by the steaming faucet,

when they strip clean, the tap water
        running black, then copper, then clear
                into the grease-clotted drain,

there's no one to witness the slap
    of a wet rag tossed in the break-
        room sink or the champ of gravel

in the empty lot. How the stars dim
    as morning comes on. How a semi downshifts
        on the overpass and the shop windows rattle

as it goes.

When Charlie Pulls the Colorado Over

When Charlie pulls the Colorado over
and tells me to fuck off, says
I can ride the bed with the bales
or hitch back to Parkton with whoever
will stop but god help him he don't
give a damn if no one does, I pull
the latch and stumble down
onto the sun-scrubbed shoulder.
The passenger door hangs open
like a jaw, hinge locked up and squealing
in the Chesapeake wind that loosens
hay strands fistfuls at a time
from the twine-tied stacks,
scatters them into traffic.
I run my thumb along the mis-
matched quarter panel, thinking
about a woman I loved who called
that morning to say she's marrying
a fighter pilot, bought a place
outside Jerusalem, that she's learned
to say *his ways are ways*
of pleasantness and she's chosen

to cover her hair and the freckled skin
of her arms –
                    halfway between
Hunt Valley and Hackensack,
the Econo Lodge sign pulsing
behind the curtain, the sounds
we make mixing with the branches
lashing the window, the rain, the big-rigs
on the interstate – *the kind of love*
that makes you forget, she says,
slipping from the sheets –
                                        and whatever
seized her then, whatever swept her
toward those distances, the Abrahamic plains,
a language she'd never spoken
but is learning, now, to speak,
is what lifts me, one foot on the bumper,
good arm levering my body into the bed.
What sets me down among the wind-
torn bales, pushes me upstate,
toward Monkton, Hereford, New Freedom,
the dropseed prairies, the runoff ponds
and feedcorn fields. What asks me
to try and track one straw, to hold it
with my eyes for more than a second,
and fail, then choose another
and fail again, Charlie leaning on the horn
as they vault into the wind.

V.F.W. Post #2046

for N.M.

She fires the boiler first thing,
cursing the pilot and Christ Jesus

and the damp matches she fumbles
in the furnace room's musty light.

Sunday, bingo night, shuttered bar,
the shining slab where my father

spent the better part of a decade
conning drinks out of regulars,

sharking the table, cracking jokes,
lined with upturned stools and rags.

For years it was a couple days
a week, him coming in dusted

with sheetrock, permanent grin,
slapping a twenty on the grain.

Then it was every other, then
every, then two-three times a day

coming in dug out and feral, fat-
faced, broad hands gone thin.

She stopped serving him then.
I've always loved her for that,

though by those days nothing
could have slowed him. I was a boy

in the booth behind, watching
as the light held still over the black-

and-white portraits, the bills signed
and tacked to the rafters.

She doesn't think of him now.
Not often. She twists the key

to the storage room. Disappears
and reappears hauling a rolling cart

of folding tables. Heaves them
onto their sides, kicks out and locks

the legs. Flips them each upright
and starts setting out the chairs.

Franklin Free Clinic

She drops the tooth
in the pan, packs my cheek
to sop the blood. I'm
telling her about the mole
on my hand I'm sure
is cancer. Runs
in my family. My aunt
with the scar smeared
between her breasts.
My grandfather's femur
riddled with it.
She tells me to relax.
I'm fine. I'm not fine
and she pretends
not to hear. I try
telling her about my ex,
the pale seam
at her throat where
after months
of mysterious sickness,
after thrush, fever, bone-
deep pain, they lifted

a mass slick
as an avocado pit.
I shape my hands
to show the largeness of it.
I tell her how I'd lie
awake at night and look.
How my own throat caught.
She pulls the cotton
from my mouth, coughs
into her elbow. Hands me
two tiny tubes of toothpaste.
One soft-bristled brush.

Safety

My brother shows me
the iron sights. The dark O
of the muzzle. The grip.
Describes the caliber,
the diameter of the holes
they hollow, how the copper
jackets bloom. Presses
its weight to my palm, says
they make the real thing
in runs of a hundred
thousand. *Ideal,* he says.
Light, and cheap. He lays
his hands on mine, steers
the open mouth toward
his window, the neighbor's
place beyond it, then
toward the bedroom where
our mother is sleeping.
I want to keep us
safe, he says. I ask what
he means. Crickets
string out their thin music

between the duplexes
and brick-front ranches
of our block. A late rain
slicks the patched-
over street. Our motion
light flickers on,
and the blacktop shines.

Close

Off early from B&R Diesel, sharp
with liquor and filtered Kings, he drifts
across the double-yellow, swings
into an iced-over lot. He runs me through
the basics: K-turn, parallel, back-in.
Jerks the Sierra into reverse and eases
the bumper up against the side
of the old bank building. We meet
at the end of the loaded bed, exhaust
and brakelight pooling around our knees.
He balls the front of my coat in his fist,
pulls me close to show the distance
between bumper and brick, pulls hard
until I'm up against the slender arc
of his collarbone, the fine dark stubble
shading his jaw, his hollowed-out cheeks.
He's still beautiful, my father. Fluid.
Powerful. His bare forearms corded
with muscle, bristling in the cold. Yes,
he's drunk. Yes, I have already begun the life-
long work of hating him, a job
that will carve me down to almost

nothing. I have already begun to catalog
every way he has failed me. Yes.
And here he is. Home early from a day shift
in Fall River. Teaching me what I need
to know. Pulling me roughly toward him,
the last half-hour of sunlight blazing
in his face, saying *This is how close
you can get.* Asking if I can see it.
If I know what he means. Saying *This. This
close. Like this.*

After the Attempt

They took your shoelaces,
your carabiner of tooth-
edged keys, but left you
your belt, which you cinched
over your loopless scrubs.

They shaved your scalp
for the stitches but missed
a tuft above your ear
that catches the light
from the hingeless windows.

The receptionist holds up
a small paper bag
stapled shut. Whatever
you had worth saving.
You look, then look away.

Once, hungover
on a gut-and-remodel job
in Grafton, you cracked the root
of your nose with your claw
hammer's backswing.

You stood very still after,
watching your blood scatter
on the plywood floor, alien
and bright as coins
from a distant country.

Vows

You said *I want to be married.*
You said *I want to be married*

to you. You said *We were children*
together. Who better?

You said *I moved for you once*
already. You said *I need this.*

You said *It will be quick.*
Backyard. July. My mother

will cook, my brother will DJ.
Here's the date. Here's the phone.

You said *There is so much*
to do: spray the bushes

with repellent, bind
these sunflowers with twine.

Hack this stump down
to a hollow, fill it with stone.

Here. Standing in July,
in the backyard, reciting the words

you wrote in ballpoint
on a scrap of ruled paper. *Here*

I am. And slowly, as if
emerging from a long sleep,

and looking around,
and confusing myself

for the cufflinks, the hushed
crowd, the white tent

billowing like a sail – I take
your hand. I start to speak.

In the Sideyard

A splinter of moon lodges deep
in the limbs of the spruce.

My brother – half my age, shivering –
lifts the splitting maul, one

smooth hand gripping the heel,
the other at the haft. The steel

he set and honed himself glints
at the crest of his practiced arc,

dividing cold from dark,
each half-log of knotted oak

from its twin. His shadow, large
as a man's, pitches headlong

into the dirt.

Dundalk

Wayne came back late from lunch, put his head down on his desk and slept. I was finishing up a lesson on supply-side economics. Noon slumped through the half-shut blinds and the classroom was hot. I knew he was high. I clicked the next slide. Turns out he was spotted ducking out at lunch, slipping behind the Sunoco on Church. School cop asked me a few leading questions then kicked him out for good. Said it was his last strike. He punched his own ticket. Next day, it's like nothing happened: the kids of south Baltimore turn to the clock, the scuffed tile floor. Snap gum in their teeth. I go back to *deadweight loss, human capital, returns on investment*. I go back to my rented rowhome on the northside where I live with a guy who ships in airtight bricks from Washington State, breaks them into eighths and makes a killing off Hopkins kids. He says stuff like *money makes money* and *cops here have bigger fish*. Some days, driving home, I go south, get halfway out on the Key Bridge and pull off. From here, you can see the waste plant's gold honeycomb towers, the faded terminals, dock cranes leaning out over the harbor like drunks. You could stay, if you wanted, for an hour, two, as long as you could stand it, watching the container ships drift in and churn out, the longshoremen offloading, shuffling the stacks. Long enough and you could watch what's left of the workday drain off into the Chesapeake. Watch night spread out like an oil slick and go still.

Michael

If we met up in the iced-over lot at the neighborhood's edge
we were kids in – grid of low-slung ranches sunk
under the lengthening shadows of larch and pine,
each street slanted toward the state building where our folks
collected their checks on the first of each month –

and if your eyes were glossed with oxys and a week
without sleep, body a loose frame of copper piping propped
under your oversized coat, and we stood, face-to-face –
Michael, what would be left between us?
What would remain of tunneling under chainlink

after the Wilsinski house burned down, slipping
between the brick pallets and front-end loaders, looking
for something to claim? Or that July we worked stripping kudzu
and poison oak from your sideyard on the promise of a few bucks
from your dad, our longsleeves matted with pine pitch and sweat?

We found a yellowjacket nest, a paper lantern buried deep
in the brake. You dared me to hit it with a Wiffle ball bat
and I did and the yellowjackets stitched my chest and arms
with fire. I came back last Christmas and sat on the hard edge
of my little brother's twin bed as he showed me how to thumb

an imaginary bullet into a handgun with REPLICA etched
on the barrel. Taught me words like breechblock
and chamber-throat. Blowback and primer. Showed me how
to switch off the safety, to keep my finger away from the trigger
until I'm ready to pull. The way your brother Daryl

took himself out of this world. I thought of you, thirteen,
weighing out nickels in your bedroom at your dad's place.
Twisting a dutchie, licking it shut. You didn't give a shit,
but I stuffed a paper towel tube with dryer sheets and we blew
our smoke through to hide the smell. All I have of you now

is rumor: a few run-ins with the cops for small stuff –
petty theft, possession – that you knocked up a girl
from Willimantic. That you were faded on cough syrup
and drifted into oncoming traffic on 84, limped away
with a sprained ankle but otherwise fine. There was a time

when I thought I knew what swerves us from disaster,
what separates us. All I can do now, Mike, is praise the state-
cut checks and the baggies of pills. Praise the quick transaction,
the no-look pass, twenty twisted into a palm. The Robitussin-
kiss, the slow drift of the wheel. The soft shoulder.

Next of Kin

A dim-eyed woman skips her meds and scales
a barb-wire fence outside Lake Charles. Five hundred
miles west, her daughter paces the faded blue outline
of a handicapped spot. The salt wind whips her hair
into her mouth. She says *what* over and over
into the phone. A voice says *torsional* and *trauma*
and *need you to decide.* The last time she saw
her mother, she found her rocking on the stoop
of her rented duplex, threading electrical wiring
through the spokes of a bicycle rim. Hair matted
and half-braided. Long fingers deftly working.
She took her inside and put her to bed. Next morning,
her mother was gone. What can you do?
The palm trees hang their heads. The wind delivers
car exhaust and brine. She has given up the parking spot.
She starts to circle the shopping cart corral.

Training

My little brother says he's worried about me.
Asks why I left my wife. We get cut off
and he calls back, says the bottoms
of his feet are finally healing up, he's back
on base, packing on muscle. Four nights
in the brackish swamps of south Georgia,
hunger-sick, stumbling, and each time one
of his squad lay prone to consult the wilted map,
he'd have to kick them awake. *Roots,* he says.
Get one jammed in your ribs and the ache
will keep you up. I tell him I found a studio
in Oakland, full-size stove, eucalyptuses
leaning prehistoric in the hills. That I climbed
one morning up under the overpass on Forest,
a little drunk, and pressed my palm to the cool
underside to feel the traffic rushing over.
I was pissing brown, he says. *I knew if I quit*
they'd give me a gallon of water, let me crash
in the jeep. But I also knew the worst of it
was done. The third night, orbs of red light
circled the cottonwood trunks. The fourth,
he spotted his first girlfriend fifty, a hundred

yards ahead. She turned slowly to face him,
then bent down to hover a pale hand
above the water. It happened over and over.
She'd bend and he'd drop his rucksack and sprint
into a clearing soaked in half-light and steam,
and see her again, turning, farther off.

Going

Alone now in San Francisco. Thin cloud rusting
over Bernal Hill, garlic simmering

in the pan, lavender potted and long dead
in the breezeway. I start the water,

carry the milk crates in from the garage.
You with your mother in Los Angeles.

The lanterns we scavenged and hung
at the ceremony now a soft racket

in the magnolia. Me turning an old
summer over, the one where we slept

most nights in a park in Hartford,
bedded down in the soaked grass.

The local kids coming always after dark
to tag the pumphouse, sling rocks

at the heron cages. Their bright
startled cries and us burrowing deeper

in our bags. I start unshelving
my books, fitting them side by side

in a crate. How one time a guard
came hollering, whipping his light

over the lawn and they took off, ditching
their backpacks, the cans, their names

silvering the brick. We watched
as they tore down the moonlit hill,

headed for the coupe they stashed
at the turnoff, bare legs flashing, the guard

close behind as they vaulted the fence
and hit the blacktop sprinting,

picking up speed – the two of us clutching
at each other, wincing, whispering.

You saying you hope they get busted.
Me hoping they get away clean.

Dry Season

It had ended and ended
badly so I'd stopped drinking
and started again or was
about to when an old friend
bought me a nonstop to stay
with him in Colorado this was early
October and the first snows
had driven the elk down
out of the upper ranges
backing up traffic into Lyons
and drawing crowds of tourists
who posed alone or with
their blonde polo'd families a safe
distance from their wildness I
watched disgusted I thought
there is nothing worse
than this shit knowing of course
that there was much worse and that I
had done it I lay down
on my friend's bottom bunk
and woke in the morning
and wandered into the living

room where vaulted windows
looked out on a parched field
and there was an elk there
then four five clustered
between boulders picking at
the stunted shrubs even larger
up close than I expected the night
before I left for good I slept
on the living room floor
and she came out shivering
and sobbing asking me
to hold her just for a minute and I
said no I said no because so
many times before I had said
yes and not meant it and just
like that I knew I was
small and cruel and moved
out across the placid bay
and shut myself up in my one-
room apartment and drank
and watched spaghetti
westerns A Fistful of Dollars
Duck You Sucker the elk
meandering closer
to the window where I stood
scowling into the light I pressed
my palm to the thick sheet
of glass between us and smacked it
once hard and not one of them

turned so I hit it again both
hands this time making a sound
like an empty plastic tub a
hollowed-out thing and the closest
lifted its head ears high
tuft of white tail twitching
and looked calmly upon me
without recognition
and went on eating the wild grasses

Kabekona

Drifting in a borrowed Old Town
on a chain-lake outside Bemidji.

Bluegills nosing the surface.
Birches and their bright silences

on the shore. Two weeks gone
and nothing is easier. Remembering

her thumb tracing my hipbone,
early sun running its hands

through our hair. The shyness
gone out of us then, all sweat

and a reckless need, pressing
hard, trying to break through

into feeling. I lean out
over the gunnel and trail my fingers,

watch the walleye flicker
in their private dark. Wanting that.

To be open-mouthed and simple.
To let the cold water touch me all over.

Farmsitting

Most days the same
with minor variations. Flat blue

of the 5 a.m. kitchen. Two scoops of feed
in a plastic bucket. A small bowl

of yogurt and an hour stacking
what the ice brought down overnight.

I was happy. I slept in their bed,
I read the mysteries on their shelves.

Always something precious gone,
someone hot on the trail.

I walked in borrowed boots
across the frozen pasture and back

each morning, each morning
the feed, the spigot, the horse dragging

its bulk against the stall.
I'd walk out nights and stand

on the same trampled spot in the yard
and listen to the cold stirring

in the cheatgrass. Dull glow of a town
on the horizon. Hiss of snow.

I'd lie in their bed under three heavy
cotton blankets and worry

about the horse and the dwindling
supplies. It was a life and it was not

mine. To sleep, I imagined the great
slabs of granite buried slantwise

in the hills. To sleep, I counted
the measures ticked out

in the porcelain tub, slow drip
to keep the pipes from freezing.

Mud Season

The road leading away from the hospital
was long, tree-lined and pocked

with shallow holes from the constant freeze
and thaw so that each time I swerved

my father's jaw flexed in the passenger
seat, though he said nothing. He was wearing

a pair of loose black jeans and an off-
white T-shirt, clean, the sleeves covering

the Celtic knotwork our neighbor
had inked clumsily around both biceps.

He pointed. I turned onto a two-lane highway,
cup change chiming, ladders shuddering

against the bolted-on racks. The sun was low
in the trees and it cut across us

in flashes, bright, then dark, then bright
again, quickly. He rested his head

on the window and I realized I had no idea
what I was supposed to do with him.

He pointed. I turned. Dense neighborhoods
gave way to fields of wild grasses. A duplex

tight to the curve of the road sprang up
alongside us: pale blue siding, a porch

that slumped heavily toward the street.
There was nowhere to pull off,

so we idled in the road. *You remember
this place?* he said. *We lived here, you and me.*

It was getting dark. Headlights winked on
across the far field. The wheel trembled

under my hands and the dash lights
made strange angles of his face.

Remember? he said. *When you were small?*

For Good

When she left
for good, turning hand

over hand
onto the interstate,

I imagine my birth
mother knew my father

wasn't bent or broke
beyond our fixing.

Just that it is enough
to want to go.

Salvage

Still somewhere in me the summer
spent driving steel into the wet earth: heft
and swing of the mattock, my blistered hands,
blackflies rising like steam. The tables
I served. The law firms I hustled
from one zipline to another, classroom
where I taught economics to the medicated
kids of bus drivers and stevedores, swept-
clean boulevards of the city that paid me
to snap a picture of every downtown
business, jot the names and hours in a spiral-
bound book. Somewhere in me the failed
industrial towns of New England
with their posh English names – Weymouth,
Bridgeport, Lowell, Worcester – their dead
cars, their factories and silk mills converted
and upsold to commuters, somewhere
the third-floor walkup we lived in
longest: cracked plaster and single-pane, plastic
paneling painted to look like real wood,
and my stepmother, my real mom, bending
over the glossy stack of Star Market mailers,

hands thin, approximate, bright scars
on the backs of her wrists where the surgeries
didn't take, and me, problem kid
with a mushroom cut and his shirt tucked
into his sweats, clipping the dollar-offs,
the half-offs, the buy-one-get-ones, the buy-one-
get-twos, the store-issued doublers, shoulder
to shoulder on the kitchen floor and the afternoon
stretching on into no kind of heaven
I could have understood then. Of peeling
linoleum and the drone of interstate traffic.
Of WIC checks, name-brand knockoffs, the gray
stamps card made to pass as a regular Visa.
Where we are allowed to know exactly what we
can have, and keep. And what it will cost.

Piecework

My grandpa was always afraid
of the machines in his shop – plunge-
router, lathe, temperamental planer
he traded for back when he was first
getting sober. Said his buddy
was doing piecework one time
at the table saw, looked up,
looked down and his right thumb
was on the floor. Hum of the cross-
cut blade, morning swelling
in the high windows. And just now,
twenty hours in, I nod off doing 80
outside Harrisburg and this
borrowed Civic goes perfectly on
without me. Quiet. Efficient.
Hands numb on the straightaway,
shorn stalks and industrial silos
sliding. I hit the rumble strip
and pull off at the Shurfine for air.
Dry flakes swirling in the fluorescent
overheads, the lot choked with cars.

No pain, he said, until later.
I blow into my hands, crack a window
and keep going. My brother ships out
in a week. It's a wide country.
I need to tell him before he goes.

My Father at 23, on the Highway
Side of an Overpass Fence

The details always the same.
Salt wind tearing at his jacket.
Bootheels dug deep

in the chainlink. The two doses
slipped under his tongue
at a friend of a friend's party

and the coming-to
blinking at a half-lit stretch
of the Long Island Expressway.

He would call me down
into the bachelor pad he made
of our basement – ratty couch,

knob-dial TV, mini-fridge
he bartered a tiling job for
stocked with Narragansett –

and tell me again about the fence,
the wind, the semis pitching
into the dark.

Even then, I didn't believe him.
This was the man who one time
told me three punk kids

mugged him for the camo jacket
I found later in the trash.
Who said he was a SEAL,

that he was shot in Da Nang
and showed me an acne scar
on his chest. Pale crater

above his left nipple. And now
that I've stacked a decade
and the width of the country

between us, now that I've chewed
a fistful of bluish stems
and sprawled out

in the soybean, slightest
stalk-sway rippling the brilliant
surfaces of my skin –

now that I know the one
where my stepmom tells him
finally to leave and he walks

calmly into the bathroom
and fills a shoebox with all
the leftover meds

and the cops pull up
and cuff him and scrawl
their badge numbers on the forms –

if he was ever up
on that overpass, it wasn't
a bad trip that put him there.

I get it. In California, in the thin
middle of my twenties, I'm up
most nights on Bernal Hill,

walking the radio tower fence-line,
measuring the distances.
The three thousand miles

between San Francisco
and the town where the shadows
of my brothers grow tall.

The cash I don't wire,
the numbers I don't dial.
The marriage that didn't survive

the summer. The version
where I'm blameless and the one
where I again abandoned

what was difficult.
Holding them each up.
Testing for nerve. For weight.

Some nights are clear
and the moon lacquers everything.
Some nights a thunderhead

scuds low across the bay,
scraping over the dock cranes
and port-locked ships,

the variegated stacks.
The headlands massing behind.
Bright traffic streaking below.

Window Washers

All day they ride the long metal box up the gleaming side
of the hospital. Rags in a plastic washtub. Squeegees
and a trough of soapy water. Below, the sidewalk fenced off,
the upturned faces gawking as they rise, ratcheting up
to the next row of windows. A man sits on a bus stop bench
and watches them work until he is ready to go in and see
what's become of his father. A man he some days comes close
to loving. He has traveled a long way to get here. He's the only
one who is coming. He will sit by his father's bed in the ward
and wait for a face to appear in the window. Wet and squinting
under a white cap. He will wait for the suds to blot out the light.
The furious churning on the other side. The soap rinsed away
as someone works the ratchet. Chest. Knees. Sneakers. Sky.

Interim

On the glassed-in back porch
of a friend's house on Folsom,

I slept three weeks on a heap
of patterned wool blankets,

a large Ziploc of granola
and a jar of pistachios on the sill.

I woke to bus traffic
in the floorboards and sun

on my face, drank thin coffee
and scoured the listings

for a studio someplace more
possible. Each day nothing

and each day I paced
the bright narrow side streets

with my friend, who was taking
time off and who was an expert

in digital currencies.
I'd tell him about the collapse

of my marriage and he'd tell me
about the distant servers

that mine electronic coins
by solving complex equations.

The specialized equipment
required for this kind of work.

I would ask him basic questions
and he would answer patiently:

The coins are encrypted code.
The code is the currency. Value

is determined by speculation.
Those days, every detail

had the glimmer of potential
cruelty: hot-pink curtain

caught in a shut window,
drainpipe signed KING BABY

in white-out pen, paper bag
of potatoes rotting in the trunk

of the car I borrowed to retrieve
a crate of books from storage.

I called a man about a place
above a Thai restaurant and lied

about how much I make in a year.
He was from Pittsburgh. We talked

about rain. He said he'd call later
to tell me if I got it. On another walk

I asked my friend more questions.
Will it replace cash? *Yes.*

Is it untraceable? *Yes.* What happens
when they run out of equations?

A bus hummed past, skimming
the lowest branches of the ficus tree

giving us shade. *It's not like that,*
he said. *It could go on forever.*

Behind the Eyes, & Shining

If I could say it once, clearly. If I could get it right.
If I could hold it all together in my mind: the pollen shook loose

like dander and the sapsucker punching holes
in the siding. The chainlink grown through birch and wind

where the ranch used to be. If I could pass my body
through the seam between shingle and ridge beam, linoleum

and plank. Return as termite, ditch weed. If I could go back
to that July in Northampton, blowing fiberglass

into rich folks' attics. To when me and Ant
let the blower run and smoked blunts all day in the trailer.

To when it was a scam and we knew it. If I could admit
it was a scam: my father's voice soft on the machine. Sober.

Asking me to call back. If I had to admit why I won't. If I had to reckon
with what the past asks of the present. If I am here

in his van. Stale cigarillo smoke and the heavy redolence
of the body. Windows fogged over. Blankets damp with rain.

If I squat against the wheelwell, and look at his quiet hands,
and do not turn away. If they tremble. If they're still.

ACKNOWLEDGMENTS

Gratitude to the editors of the following journals and magazines in whose pages these poems first appeared, sometimes in a different form:

Adroit: "Deciding." *AGNI:* "Natick," "Window Washers." *Arcadia:* "Graduation." *Bat City Review:* "Free Armchair, Worcester," "Dundalk." *Blackbird:* "Brothers." *The Cortland Review:* "When Charlie Pulls the Colorado Over." *Devil's Lake:* "Blue." *Forklift, Ohio:* "Behind the Eyes, & Shining," "Next of Kin." *Gulf Coast:* "After the Attempt." *Indiana Review:* "After the Hurricane," "My Father at 49, Working the Night Shift at B&R Diesel." *The Journal:* "The First Time." *The Missouri Review:* "Graffiti." *Narrative:* "Close," "My Father at 23, on the Highway Side of an Overpass Fence." *New England Review:* "In the Supply Closet at Illing Middle." *Passages North:* "Workbench." *Ploughshares:* "Interim." *Redivider:* "Tap Out." *The Sewanee Review:* "Piecework," "Franklin Free Clinic," "Going," "Michael," "Safety."

"After the Hurricane" was featured at the NEA Writer's Corner.
"My Father at 49 . . ." was chosen by Tracy K. Smith for inclusion in *Best New Poets 2015.*

"Free Armchair, Worcester" was chosen by Natalie Diaz for inclusion in *Best New Poets 2017*.

––––––––––

This book would not have been possible without the support of the National Endowment for the Arts, the Creative Writing Program at Stanford University, the MFA program at Vanderbilt University, the Kratz Center for Creative Writing at Goucher College, the Bread Loaf Writers' Conference, the Sewanee Writers' Conference, and the MacDowell Colony. Thank you to the hardworking folks who keep these institutions alive and well.

Unending thanks to my teachers & mentors Elizabeth Spires, Mark Jarman, Eavan Boland, Louise Glück, Ken Fields, Rick Hilles, Beth Bachmann, Pete Fairchild, Ann Christie, Edward Hirsch, Tom Sleigh, Kate Daniels, Stephen Rascher, David Lang, Adam Ross, Eduardo C. Corral, Carl Phillips, and Rick Barot – and to my very first poetry teacher, Steve Straight, whose sharpness and generosity encouraged me to pursue a life in language.

To fellow writers & dear friends Tiana Clark, Will Brewer, Ryann Stevenson, Chris Drangle, Emma Catherine Perry, Noah Warren, Grady Chambers, Margaret Ross, Kai Carlson-Wee, Javier Zamora, Mikko Harvey, Matthew Kelsey, Laura Romeyn, Keith Leonard, Kien Lam, Ari Banias, Solmaz Sharif, Brian Tierney, Kara Krewer, Will Schutt, Michael Lee, Janet Thielke, Claire Jimenez, Ricardo Zamarano Baez, Anessa Ibrahim, Justin Boening, Cate Lycurgus, Chad Abushanab, Josh Kalscheur, Phillip B. Williams, Sam Ross, and Ben Naka-Hasebe Kingsley.

To my workshop-mates at Vanderbilt and Stanford, especially Chris Adamson, Cara Dees, Dan Haney, Alicia Brandewie, Anne

Charlton, Sara Strong, Max McDonough, Simone Wolff, Mary Somerville, Charif Shanahan, J. Bruce Fuller, Casey Thayer, Nick Friedman, and Essy Stone.

To my family, especially Rowena and Jim, Linda and Tim, Nancy, Sharon, the King and Queen, Rob, Jason, Larry and Dora, Jessie and Tom, Evil Auntie Sue, Camma, Cheryl and Joe, Zack, Carole, Greg, Cathy and Steve, Bill and Teresa, Otto and Karen, Jim and Nivin, Meme and Pepe, Grandpa K – and to all my cousins, blood or otherwise.

To my mom, Suzanne, and my brothers, Luke and Noah, whose love has saved me many times over.

To my father, Christopher, who cared for me when I was a baby.

To my brilliant editor, Jenny Xu, whose ideas shaped this book profoundly, and to the HMH crew who worked tirelessly on its behalf.

To Anders Carlson-Wee, whose steadfast friendship has meant the world. Here's to many more years working side by side in the shop.

And to my sweetheart, the radiant Katie Moulton, without whom none of this would mean a thing.